T0015893

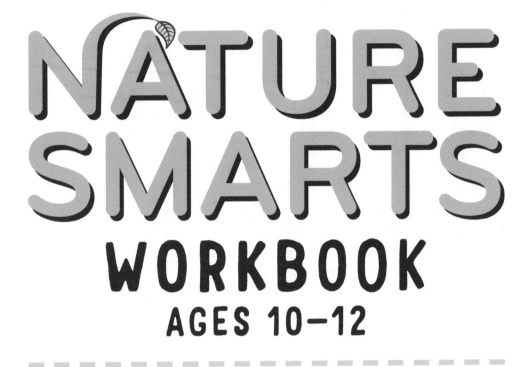

NATURE SMARTS

WORKBOOK

AGES 10–12

From the
Environmental
Educators of
Mass Audubon

Storey Publishing

The mission of Storey Publishing is to serve our customers by publishing practical information that encourages personal independence in harmony with the environment.

Edited by Deanna F. Cook and Hannah Fries
Art direction and book design by Michaela Jebb
Text production by Jennifer Jepson Smith
Illustrations by © Jada Fitch

Text © 2023 by Massachusetts Audubon Society, Inc.

All rights reserved. No part of this book may be reproduced without written permission from the publisher, except by a reviewer who may quote brief passages or reproduce illustrations in a review with appropriate credits; nor may any part of this book be reproduced, stored in a retrieval system, or transmitted in any form or by any means—electronic, mechanical, photocopying, recording, or other—without written permission from the publisher.

The information in this book is true and complete to the best of our knowledge. All recommendations are made without guarantee on the part of the author or Storey Publishing. The author and publisher disclaim any liability in connection with the use of this information.

Storey books are available at special discounts when purchased in bulk for premiums and sales promotions as well as for fund-raising or educational use. Special editions or book excerpts can also be created to specification. For details, please send an email to special.markets@hbgusa.com.

Storey Publishing
210 MASS MoCA Way
North Adams, MA 01247
storey.com

Storey Publishing, LLC is an imprint of Workman Publishing Co., Inc., a subsidiary of Hachette Book Group, Inc., 1290 Avenue of the Americas, New York, NY 10104

Distributed in Europe by Hachette Livre, 58 rue Jean Bleuzen, 92 178 Vanves Cedex, France
Distributed in the United Kingdom by Hachette Book Group, UK, Carmelite House, 50 Victoria Embankment, London EC4Y 0DZ

ISBN: 978-1-63586-398-7 (paper)

Printed in China by R. R. Donnelley
10 9 8 7 6 5 4 3 2 1

Library of Congress Cataloging-in-Publication Data on file

CONTENTS

Observe
Your World

You are holding this book because you are curious by nature, and curious about nature.

If you already know a lot about nature, including plants, animals, and natural processes, and you would like to build your skills so you could become a naturalist or field biologist, this book is for you. If you like exploring outside and just want to learn more, this book is for you, too!

It's best to start with the first chapter, Being a Naturalist, so you can begin to build your observation skills, but after that, feel free to hop into any chapter that interests you. Like a path you might take through a forest, you can choose your own adventure.

After you use this workbook, keep making observations and recording them in your field journal (see page 16). Becoming a naturalist means revisiting and observing places and organisms and habitats multiple times and over long periods, sometimes even years. And that's where the magic happens—you will get so good at observing that you will see amazing things that other people walk right past . . . because you have nature smarts!

Every chapter also includes an opportunity for you to use your nature smarts to make a difference by being a community scientist. You'll learn about ways to share your data and observations with scientists and how to participate in projects that help specific species.

Ready? Let's get started!

NATURALIST: a person who studies nature, observing plants, animals, and nonliving things like rocks, soil, and weather so they can better understand the natural world

Being a Naturalist

The most fundamental skill of the naturalist is observation. A naturalist is always observing—using ALL of their senses to take in information about the world that surrounds them—whether they are in a forest, at the beach, in a neighborhood park, or on a busy city street. Naturalists look for patterns and make connections between what they observe and what they already know. It seems simple, but observation is a skill that takes lots of practice.

Naturalists ask lots of questions!

Nature Observation Concentration

There are 12 natural objects on this field station table. Observe them closely, looking for patterns and other ways to remember what you see. Then turn the page and try to list all the objects. To challenge yourself, limit your observation time to 20 or 30 seconds.

➤ Ready to observe? Set your timer. Go!!

LIST AND DESCRIBE as many objects as you can remember from the previous page. After one attempt, get a fresh piece of paper, turn back to the observation page, and try again. Raise or lower your time limit, depending on how it went on the first try. You can also use a different memory strategy.

Observation 1

Plant part: _____

_____   _____

_____   _____

_____   _____

_____   _____

_____   _____

_____   _____

➤ **Reflect:** It's good practice to think about what worked well. What strategy helped you observe and remember the objects?

_____

_____

_____

_____

_____

Seeing versus Observing

When you are exploring outside, rather than simply taking in what you see, be an active observer. Use your senses to learn about different characteristics of the things around you. Try asking yourself questions related to your senses. How does an object feel? What color is it? What does it smell like?

➤ Let's practice! First, find a natural object, living or nonliving. It can be anything. Then, using descriptive language, write down the characteristics of your natural object in the spaces below.

Texture

_____

_____

_____

_____

Color

_____

_____

_____

_____

Shape

_____

_____

_____

_____

Smell

_____

_____

_____

_____

Your observations might differ from another person's. Try sharing your object with someone else and comparing how you each experience it.

Other characteristics

_____

_____

_____

What's in Your Nature Field Kit?

When you head outside, don't forget your field exploration supplies.

➤ Use this word search to discover all the helpful things you can put in your backpack!

```
C L M C H K N Q U M Y W N R A
O O I A N F H B U J U A O F Q
Q F L E G D P C W S H T T U H
O I P O F N M O M W V E R T
D E P D R Z I U E B F R B T B
E L Y H V E V F J Y F B O R R
V D M Y K C D X I N O O O S U
S G I K S H S P Q E E T K E L
G U I C B N F K E J R T G X E
S I H J A T A G S N D L R S R
U D J J Z M A C H E C E T G J
X E D O T M E S K P H I J O Z
R H D E T Z I R C S Q K L U S
F O I X Z P P E A C Z R F S H
H F I R S T A I D K I T W D H
```

NOTEBOOK   MAGNIFIER   WATER BOTTLE

PEN   FIELD GUIDE   SNACKS

RULER   CAMERA   FIRST AID KIT

COLORED PENCILS

Sensory Scavenger Hunt

Grab your field kit and head outdoors. See if you can complete this sensory scavenger hunt in a neighborhood park, a field, or your own backyard.

➤ Describe each object you find on the lines provided.

Something bumpy

Something that makes a sound

Something smooth

Something furry
(not necessarily an animal)

Something crunchy

Something that smells

Something colorful

Compare & Contrast

Find two similar natural objects, such as two leaves, two rocks, or two cones. If you can't get outside, look inside your home. Do you have a houseplant that you can use to compare two leaves? You can even use two apples or two strawberries!

➤ Use the boxes below to make a detailed drawing of each object. You can also add words to describe them.

OBJECT A

OBJECT B

How are the two objects similar?

_____

_____

_____

How are the two objects different?

_____

_____

_____

After your close observation of these two objects,
what questions do you have about them?

_____

_____

_____

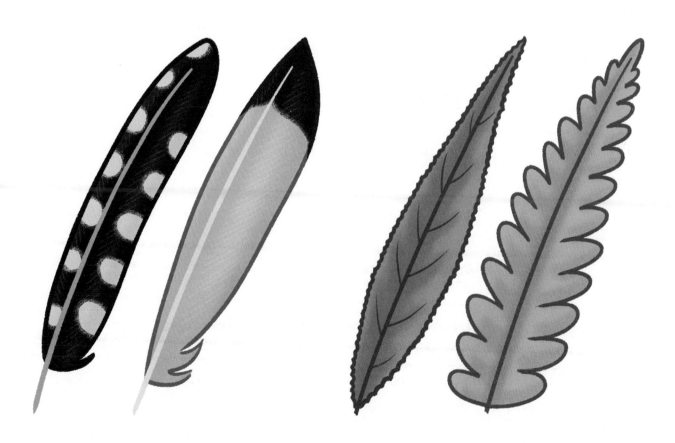

Observation or Inference?

An OBSERVATION is information that you take in through your senses. An INFERENCE is an interpretation or conclusion based on the observations you have made. Close observers develop inferences based on the data they gather from their observations.

It's important to remember that an inference is not necessarily a fact, and it is not always correct—nor does it need to be. The cool thing about inferences is that they can be turned into science investigations.

➤ Practice telling the different between an observation and an inference. Circle the "O" next to the statements below that are observations. Circle the "I" next to the inferences.

O / I   **The plant is droopy.**

O / I   **The plant needs more water.**

O / I   **The bird is singing.**

O / I   **The sky is cloudy.**

O / I   **It is going to rain soon.**

O / I   **The tracks in the sand have five toes.**

O / I   **The grass is very wet because it rained.**

➤ Take a look at the drawing below and write down three observations and three inferences about what you observe in this habitat.

Observations

1. A bird is sitting on a nest.

2.

3.

Inferences

1. There are eggs in the nest.

2.

3.

What's a Field Journal?

Scientists who work in the "field" (outside in the natural world) keep some kind of field journal. These small books usually fit easily in a backpack or pocket. They might be paper books, or they might be tablets that can also take photos and connect to online databases. A field journal is a place to record observations through descriptions, drawings, and notes. Here's just one example of what one might look like.

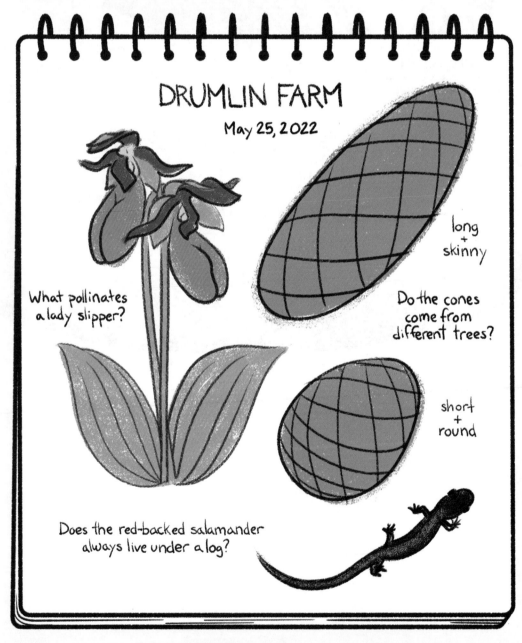

DRUMLIN FARM
May 25, 2022

What pollinates a lady slipper?

long + skinny

Do the cones come from different trees?

short + round

Does the red-backed salamander always live under a log?

Design Your Own

Every naturalist needs a field journal! How will you
design yours? Lay out a sample page below:

➤ *Here are few things you might want to record every
time you use your journal.*

- » Location
- » Date
- » Time of day
- » Weather conditions

- » Notes, descriptions, and
  drawings of your observations
- » Questions to explore further
  the next time you are out

Transects & Quadrats

When naturalists or field biologists want to know more about what kinds of and how many organisms (plants or animals) are in an area, they use transects and quadrats.

A TRANSECT is a line across a habitat. You "run" a transect by placing a cord or rope on the ground. If you want the line to stay in place over time so you can revisit your transect, you can secure it with stakes. Transects are generally used to record changes in the populations of organisms along the length of the transect line.

A QUADRAT is a square of a chosen size placed in a habitat, sometimes along a transect. Scientists study the kinds and numbers of species in the quadrat to learn more about the area they are studying.

YOU WILL NEED

A brightly colored rope approximately 10 to 20 yards/meters long

Eight stakes made of wood or PVC

String or flagging tape

Tape measure

Make Your Own Field Study

Is there a place near you where you want to take a closer look? Run a transect and create a quadrat to learn what is happening in that habitat! See the instructions on the next page.

QUADRAT

TRANSECT

Directions for Making
a Transect and a Quadrat

1　Find a place to run a transect line. If you have
room, run the transect for 10 to 20 yards
or meters so you can explore changes over
a distance. For example: from a yard to a
garden or forested area, or from the edge of
a pond outward.

2　Explore your transect line. The transect is
there to focus your attention. In your field
journal, record details about where your
transect is located (habitats, natural features,
water, etc.). Take notes about what you
observe along your line.

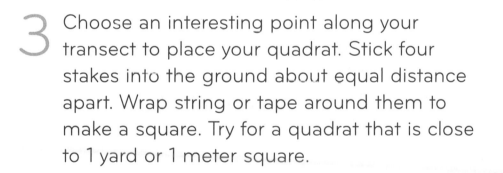

3 Choose an interesting point along your transect to place your quadrat. Stick four stakes into the ground about equal distance apart. Wrap string or tape around them to make a square. Try for a quadrat that is close to 1 yard or 1 meter square.

4 Record your observations of the quadrat. What is the soil like? Are there any plants? Invertebrates such as ants or spiders? Any signs of other animals?

5 Make a second quadrat at another point on your transect. What do you observe?

NATURALIST'S TIP

It's really up to you how much you want to explore! If you want to study a mossy area in the forest, you might want a very short transect and a smaller quadrat.

BE A COMMUNITY
SCIENTIST!

You (Yes, You!) Can Help Scientists with Real Research

COMMUNITY SCIENCE is science done by anybody, anywhere. Data collected by community scientists can help professional scientists answer research questions about animal or plant populations and habitats or about environmental factors like water temperature, air quality, or precipitation. Conservation efforts need to be based on lots of data collected over long periods of time. With the help of community scientists like you, researchers can gather much more data than they could working by themselves.

iNATURALIST is one of the easiest ways to submit data that can then be used by researchers all over the world. To set up an account, go to iNaturalist.org. Then you can download the iNaturalist app to a smartphone or tablet. iNaturalist is also a fun way to learn to identify the images of invertebrates or plants or anything else you submit, all while contributing to a global database.

CLIMATE CONNECTION

Understanding climate change and its impact on our world requires data. By helping to collect critical data, community scientists can contribute to local and global efforts to better understand climate change and make informed decisions for the future. As climate change continues to affect ecosystems around the world, more and more community science projects are being developed to collect important data for research and public policy.

Plants Where You Are

What makes a plant a plant? Most plants photosynthesize, have rigid cell walls and an outer covering or cuticle, and reproduce by making seeds or spores. Scientists who study plants are called **botanists**.

Plant Anatomy

The plants we observe in our homes, at the park, or in a forest all have the following parts.

FLOWERS or CONES are the reproductive structures of the plant. Plants can have both male and female parts or be only male or only female.

A STEM or TRUNK holds the plant up and carries water and sap from roots to leaves and back.

In woody plants and trees, the protective BARK is the outermost layer of stems and roots.

Sometimes seeds are located inside of a FRUIT. The fruit is the plant's way of distributing seeds by having an animal eat the fruit and poop the seeds out.

LEAVES or NEEDLES are where most photosynthesis happens, capturing the energy of the sun and creating the sugar molecules that the plant needs to grow.

SEEDS contain a plant embryo and stored food. Once the seed germinates, the embryo uses the energy in the stored food until it grows enough to be able to photosynthesize on its own.

ROOTS anchor the plant in the ground, absorb water and nutrients from the soil, and store sugars and starch made by the leaves.

There's a Plant Part for That!

Assign plant parts to systems in YOUR body that serve a similar function. Some plant parts may fulfill roles in more than one system. Write about how each plant part is like the system you matched it to.

 Circulatory system   Plant part: _Stem/Trunk_

The stem and trunk carry water and sap through the tree like veins carry blood through the body.

 Skeletal system   Plant part: _____

_____

_____

 Digestive system   Plant part: _____

_____

_____

 Integumentary system *(your skin, nails, and hair)*   Plant part: _____

_____

_____

A Tree by Its Bark

Bark is the protective covering of a woody plant such as a tree or shrub. The patterns and color of bark are unique to each species of tree. With some careful looking and practice, you can identify different types of trees by their bark.

➤ **How many varieties of bark can you find near you?**

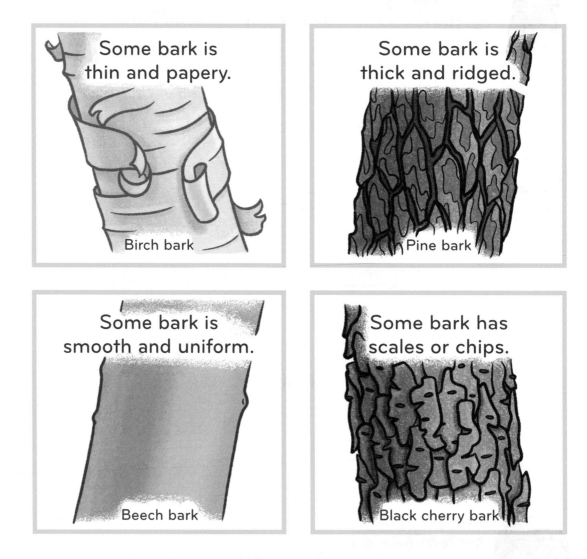

Some bark is thin and papery.

Birch bark

Some bark is thick and ridged.

Pine bark

Some bark is smooth and uniform.

Beech bark

Some bark has scales or chips.

Black cherry bark

Make Bark Rubbings

For this activity, you need three pieces of blank paper and a few crayons with the paper peeled off. Go outside and find three different types of trees. Holding the paper against the bark, rub the side of the crayon over the paper until an impression of the bark comes through.

➤ Write down your observations of your bark rubbings.

Bark #1 observation:

Bark #2 observation:

Bark #3 observation:

How are your three bark rubbings the same? How are they different? Can you distinguish between all three?

Unbe-leaf-able!

Leaves come in lots of different shapes, and every species of plant has its own distinctive leaf. Just take a look around to see how many different varieties of leaves there are!

➤ **The more you observe the leaves around you, the more details you'll notice. Try finding leaves of different shapes and textures in your neighborhood.**

Maple leaves are broad with short, pointed lobes and look sort of like the palm of your hand.

Pine needles are arranged in bunches while fir and spruce needles are attached to the branch one by one.

Clovers look like they have three leaves, but it's really one compound leaf with three leaflets.

FUN FACT!

Did you know that the oldest Great Basin bristlecone pine is over 5,000 years old?

Leaf Shape Scavenger Hunt

Can you find leaves near you that match the following shapes?

☐ 3 lobes

☐ 5 points

☐ Multiple lobes

☐ Long needles

☐ Fan shape

☐ Long and thin

☐ Sharp point

☐ Short and spiky

☐ Compound

☐ Scales

☐ Feathery

☐ Toothed edge

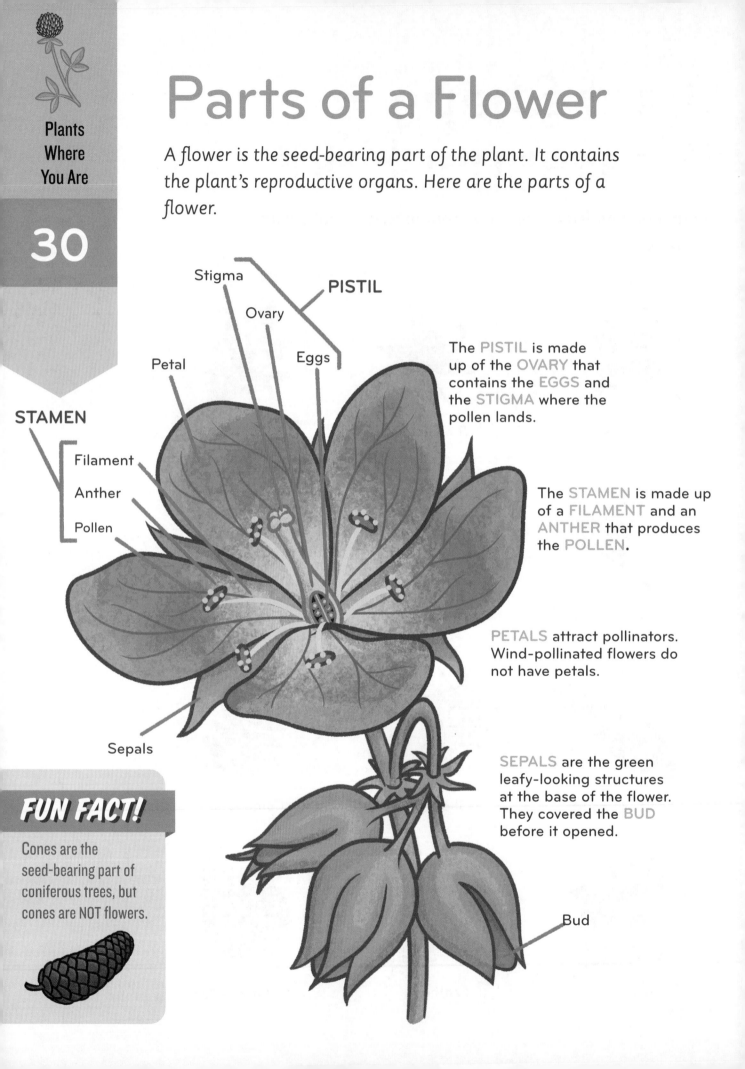

Parts of a Flower

A flower is the seed-bearing part of the plant. It contains the plant's reproductive organs. Here are the parts of a flower.

Stigma

PISTIL

Ovary

Petal

Eggs

STAMEN

Filament

Anther

Pollen

Sepals

Bud

The PISTIL is made up of the OVARY that contains the EGGS and the STIGMA where the pollen lands.

The STAMEN is made up of a FILAMENT and an ANTHER that produces the POLLEN.

PETALS attract pollinators. Wind-pollinated flowers do not have petals.

SEPALS are the green leafy-looking structures at the base of the flower. They covered the BUD before it opened.

FUN FACT!

Cones are the seed-bearing part of coniferous trees, but cones are NOT flowers.

Flower Power Word Search

```
F X T Q I P Y M O P I S T I L
P L O A V M W S B G P X T S R
G I O D V J O P T T J L K F U
J F S W A K U C K I T F E N N
G S A T E N P J U J G A H B P
R M S U A R T E M Q H M W E B
A T E K R M G H T L N F A N U
I G J G G P E C E A D S N W D
U H Q R G Z O N T R L E P X T
S B P Y O Q W L J C P P G T E
B H O V A R Y Y L J O A L K D
F I L A M E N T I E X L N R B
H T V M K D V F K Q N X V G I
R X O Z O S W B X B P M N R Z
E R I K G K Y I Q L Y Z B K J
```

FLOWER	POLLEN	STIGMA
STAMEN	PISTIL	PETAL
FILAMENT	OVARY	SEPAL
ANTHER	EGG	BUD

Flower Focus

Go on a search for flowers. A flower might be tiny and barely noticeable, or colorful and flashy. Even grasses have flowers! You can look in a garden or meadow, along the edges of the yard, or alongside a sidewalk or road.

➤ **Choose at least two different flowers to examine more closely.**

1 Examine each flower carefully by pulling it apart or using a paring knife (ask an adult to help).

2 Use the flower diagram on page 30 to help find and identify the female parts and male parts of the flower. If the flower is small, you may want to use a magnifying glass!

3 If you are looking at a flower with petals, count the petals and note the shape. Compare the structure and parts of each flower.

Compare Your Flowers

Draw each of your flowers and label all the parts you can identify.

FLOWER #1

FLOWER #2

Number of petals:

Number of petals:

Observations:

Observations:

How are your two flowers the same or different?

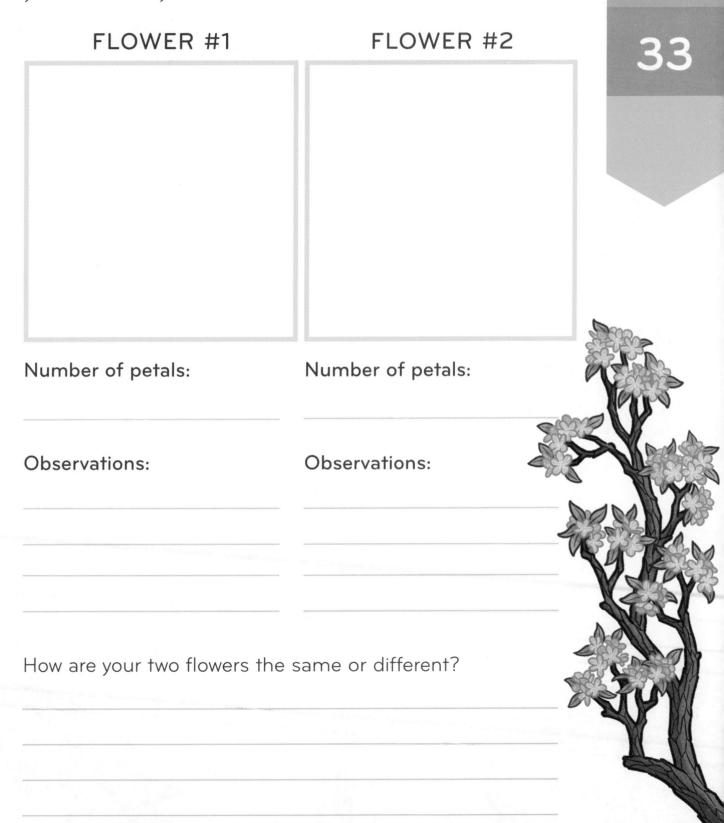

Seed Search

Seeds come in many different shapes and sizes! Try this fun investigation to find out why.

➤ First, head outside and look for up to four different types of seeds. Tape them onto the spaces below.

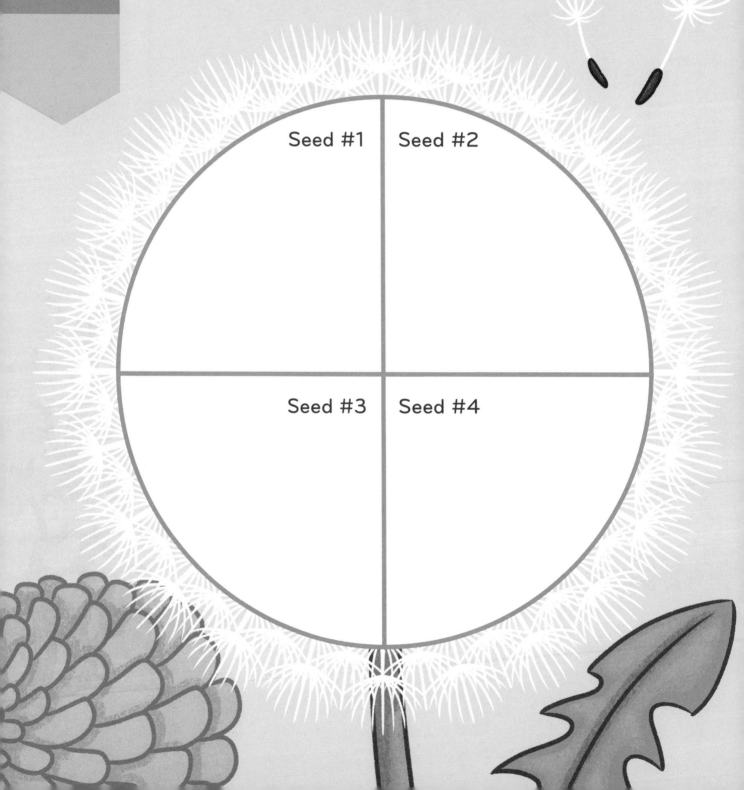

Seed #1   Seed #2

Seed #3   Seed #4

Make Your Predictions!

Examine your seeds. What are their characteristics?
Make a check mark for each description that applies.

	HARD	SOFT	HOOKS	FUZZY	WINGS	JUICY
Seed #1						
Seed #2						
Seed #3						
Seed #4						

SEEDS NEED TO BE ON THE MOVE. There are many
different ways for them to disperse, or find a space where
they can grow. Based on your observations, try to predict
how your seeds would travel. Would they float on water?
Be carried by the wind?

	CARRIED BY WIND	FLOAT ON WATER	DROP TO GROUND	STICK TO ANIMAL	EATEN BY ANIMAL
Seed #1					
Seed #2					
Seed #3					
Seed #4					

Create a Seed

*Think about the different methods seeds use for dispersal.
Can you design an imaginary seed using what you know?*

➤ Describe or illustrate a unique seed for each of the
following dispersal methods.

Travel by water (sink or float):

Travel by wind (float, twirl, or get propelled):

Travel by animal (attach or get eaten or buried):

Pick one of your seed designs and make a sculpture of it using materials you find around the house. Try letting your seed travel!

Does it float, twirl, or stick the way you imagined?

_____

_____

_____

_____

_____

_____

BE A COMMUNITY SCIENTIST!

Help Scientists Learn about How Climate Change Is Affecting Plant Life Cycles

PHENOLOGY is the study of seasonal events and when they happen. The timing of a plant's life cycle—leaves opening in spring and dropping in fall, flowers opening, seeds and fruit ripening—is all related to climate and weather.

BUDBURST is a community science project organized by the Chicago Botanic Garden. It is focused on the research question of how climate change is affecting plant phenology. You can be a part of this research by going to Budburst.org and contributing data on when the leaves and flowers appear on the plants in your area in spring and when they lose their leaves in fall.

CLIMATE CONNECTION

All plants need water and sunlight and good growing temperatures in order to thrive. Exactly how much of each depends on the plant and the climate it's adapted to. A cactus that grows in the desert has adapted to survive on very little precipitation. In fact, few cacti can live in areas with lots of rain. Aspen trees grow in areas with long, cold winters, while oak trees are adapted to areas with milder winters. Some types of aspens and oaks can live in the same area when the conditions that suit them overlap.

Being aware of the climate and weather where you live helps you know about what kinds of plants might be living there. What is the climate like where you live? What is the average yearly precipitation? What parts of the year are the wettest or driest? How hot does it get in summer? How cold in winter?

Invertebrates Where You Are

Invertebrates are animals without backbones. There are many more invertebrates in the world than vertebrates (animals with a backbone, like birds, mammals, and reptiles). Invertebrates are easy to find in every kind of habitat. In fact, you have probably found invertebrates in and around your home.

Many invertebrates are so tiny that they can only be seen with a microscope. Some, like insects, spiders, lobsters, and clams, have a hard outer covering. Others have no hard covering, like earthworms, caterpillars, and jellyfish.

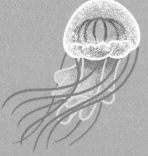

The ocean is full of invertebrates of all shapes and sizes!

Invertebrate Matchup

Invertebrates can be classified into several main categories called phyla. Read the descriptions of each of the phyla below.

➤ Next to each invertebrate on the next page, write the number of the phylum to which it belongs.

1

MOLLUSK
has a soft body, often with a shell

2

ARTHROPOD
has an exoskeleton and jointed legs

3

ANNELID
has a long, segmented, wormlike body

4

ECHINODERM
lives in water, has radial symmetry and spines or spiny skin

5

CNIDARIA
lives in water, has stinging cells

6

PORIFERA
lives in water, has a spongy body, water moves through its pores

NATURALIST'S TIP

Arthropoda is the largest phylum in the animal kingdom. Three of the animals on page 41 are arthropods!

Sea sponge _____

Spider _____

Invertebrates
Where
You Are

41

Answer
key on
page 110

Worm _____

Millipede _____

Snail _____

Lobster _____

Sea anemone _____

Sea star _____

Invert Detective Work

Most invertebrates—sometimes called inverts—are small and move quickly or spend much of their time hiding. Observing them takes patience and careful looking. If you are inside, find a spot that is not often disturbed, such as a windowsill, near a houseplant, or under a bed. If you are outside, look for a spot that has some plants growing. You may not see an invertebrate right away, but you will likely find signs of them.

➤ **Check the box if you see any of these signs of invertebrates!**

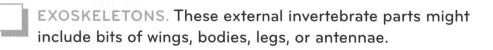

☐ **WEBS OR WEBBING.** Invertebrates make all kinds of webby stuff, from intricate spiderwebs to single strands so fine they are almost invisible.

☐ **DEBRIS PILES.** Insect scat, called frass, looks like tiny grains of sand or bits of wood. Earthworms leave piles of scat at the tops of their holes that look like tiny coiled ropes of soil.

☐ **EXOSKELETONS.** These external invertebrate parts might include bits of wings, bodies, legs, or antennae.

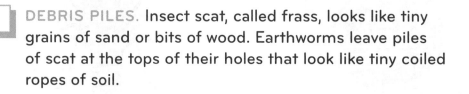

☐ **HOLES.** Many insects chew through leaves or wood and leave a hole or tunnel.

☐ **STRUCTURES.** Some insects lay eggs that form bumps on leaves or stems that are called galls. On a windowsill or along a branch you might find a shelter built of bits of grass or mud.

Follow the Signs

Once you find some evidence, return to that spot a few times to look for the invertebrates that left the signs you found. When observing, it's best to stay as quiet and as still as possible.

➤ *Sketch your invertebrate here.*

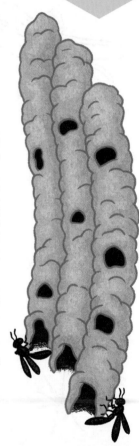

What do you observe about the invertebrate's behavior?

Can you make any inferences about what it is doing?

FUN FACT!

The insect that makes the nest above is called an organ pipe mud dauber!

Invertebrates
Where
You Are

44

Answer
key on
page 110

Invertebrate Crossword

Complete this crossword puzzle using what you know about invertebrates. If you get stuck, look it up!

The crossword grid contains 1 Down spelling ARTHROPODS vertically, with 4 Across starting at P.

ACROSS

2. The most numerous insects in the world

4. A land-based crustacean that lives under logs and curls up in a ball when disturbed

7. A tasty invertebrate with a hard shell that lives in the Atlantic Ocean

8. A soft-bodied, shelled creature

9. A common member of the arachnid group

DOWN

1. Group of inverts with an external shell

3. The name for a worm's type of body

5. A many-legged invertebrate

6. The process by which a caterpillar turns into a butterfly

Spying for Inverts

If you can go outdoors on a warm, calm day, head out and search for flowering plants. Sit quietly and watch for invertebrates that come to the flowers or are on the plant near the flowers.

➤ Use the table below to keep track of the different kinds of invertebrates you see, how many of each type, what they are doing, how long they stay, and any interactions between them.

INVERTEBRATE	QUANTITY	ACTIONS/INTERACTIONS	LENGTH OF STAY

Write about one of the invertebrates you find. Describe its body, behavior, and habitat. Can you identify it using a field guide or app?

What's My Niche?

The important role that an animal plays in the place where it lives is called its NICHE. For example, one important ecosystem niche for bees is to pollinate plants.

➤ Pick an invertebrate that interests you. Through observations and what you know about this species, can you predict what that animal's role, or niche, is in its ecosystem?

NATURALIST'S TIP

Invertebrates do many jobs that benefit humans, from pollinating flowers to decomposing dead stuff to controlling pest populations. One clue to your invertebrate's niche might be what it eats . . . or what eats it.

Invertebrate:

Prediction of its niche:

Why do you think this is the niche of your selected invertebrate?

Invert Search & Find

Can you find and circle all 11 invertebrates hiding in this picture?

BE A COMMUNITY
SCIENTIST

Help Track Monarch Butterflies on Their Great Migration

Every fall, most monarch butterflies fly from all across the United States to spend the winter in Mexico. In spring, it takes multiple generations of monarchs to migrate back north. These insects are most vulnerable during their long migrations. MONARCH WATCH, monarchwatch.org, is a community science project that studies the migration of monarch butterflies and how well they are surviving in different areas of the country. By joining Monarch Watch, you can contribute data about the monarchs near you.

CLIMATE CONNECTIONS

Monarchs are not adapted to cold temperatures and would not be able to survive the winter in most of the United States, which is why they migrate south to Mexico. With climate change making winters warmer and seasonal transitions more erratic, monarchs (and other wildlife) may not be able to understand the environmental cues they need to migrate and return safely. Also, if local summer weather becomes more extreme—droughts, major storms, extended heat waves— monarchs and their larvae will be in even greater danger.

Herptiles Where You Are

The term **herptile** is a word used when talking about both reptiles and amphibians. Even though reptiles and amphibians are very different, scientists often lump them together as a group. The study of herptiles is called **herpetology**. If you are a biologist who studies reptiles and amphibians, you might say to other folks, "I study herps!"

What's a Herptile?

Most herptiles have a head, body, tail, and four legs . . . but not all of them. Here are some of the most common reptiles and amphibians.

➤ Check them off if you think some of them live near you, then look online to see if you were right.

❏ SNAKES are reptiles with a head, a very long, narrow body, a tail, and no legs. Snakes do not have ears, but they can sense vibrations. They have distinctive colors and patterns.

❏ TURTLES are reptiles with a two-part shell—the carapace on top and the plastron underneath. Turtles have no teeth. They have internal ears.

❏ LIZARDS are reptiles, too. They have scaly skin and often have color patterns that you can learn to recognize.

FROG

TOAD

❏ **FROGS AND TOADS**
are amphibians. They have
large mouths, eyes on top of
their heads, large back legs
for jumping, and no tails.
Frogs have smooth, wet or
damp skin while toads have
bumpy, dry skin.

ALLIGATOR

CROCODILE

❏ **ALLIGATORS AND
CROCODILES** are large
reptiles with long snouts
and tails and short limbs.
American crocodiles have
a narrower snout than
American alligators, and
both upper and lower teeth
are visible when the mouth
is closed. Never approach an
alligator or crocodile—yikes!

FUN FACT!

Alligators can grow up
to 18 feet long!

❏ **SALAMANDERS** are
small amphibians with long
bodies and tails and short
legs. Their skin is smooth
and wet or damp. They can
often be identified by their
spot patterns.

Salamander Life Cycles

Amphibians are cold-blooded vertebrates that live in fresh water and on land. Examples of amphibians include frogs, toads, and salamanders. You probably know all about the life cycle of a frog or toad.

BUT WHAT ABOUT A SALAMANDER? Check out the fun facts below.

Many species of salamanders, like red-spotted newts, lay their eggs in ponds. When they hatch they look a lot like tadpoles except that they have frilly gills.

The aquatic adults move back to the water, where they mate and lay eggs, completing the life cycle.

Some species of salamanders, such this red-backed salamander, have adapted to laying eggs in moist terrestrial settings and spend their entire lives on land.

In the water, red-spotted newts change into a juvenile stage called efts and move onto land, where they live under moist leaves and decaying logs.

FUN FACT!

Newts belong to the Salamandridae family. The word *salamander* is the name for this large group of amphibians. Here's the tricky part: All newts are salamanders, but not all salamanders are newts.

Efts live on land for a couple years until they transform once again.

Herptiles
Where
You Are

54

Answer
key on
page 110

Land or Water?

Where would you find each of these amphibian life stages in the habitat pictured at right? A is land, B is both land and water, and C is water.

➤ Write the letter that corresponds to the correct place. Remember to check the salamander life cycle on pages 52 and 53!

_____C_____ FROG EGGS

_____ FROG TADPOLES

_____ ADULT FROG

_____ RED-BACKED
SALAMANDER EGGS

_____ AQUATIC
ADULT NEWT

_____ RED-SPOTTED
NEWT EGGS

_____ RED EFT

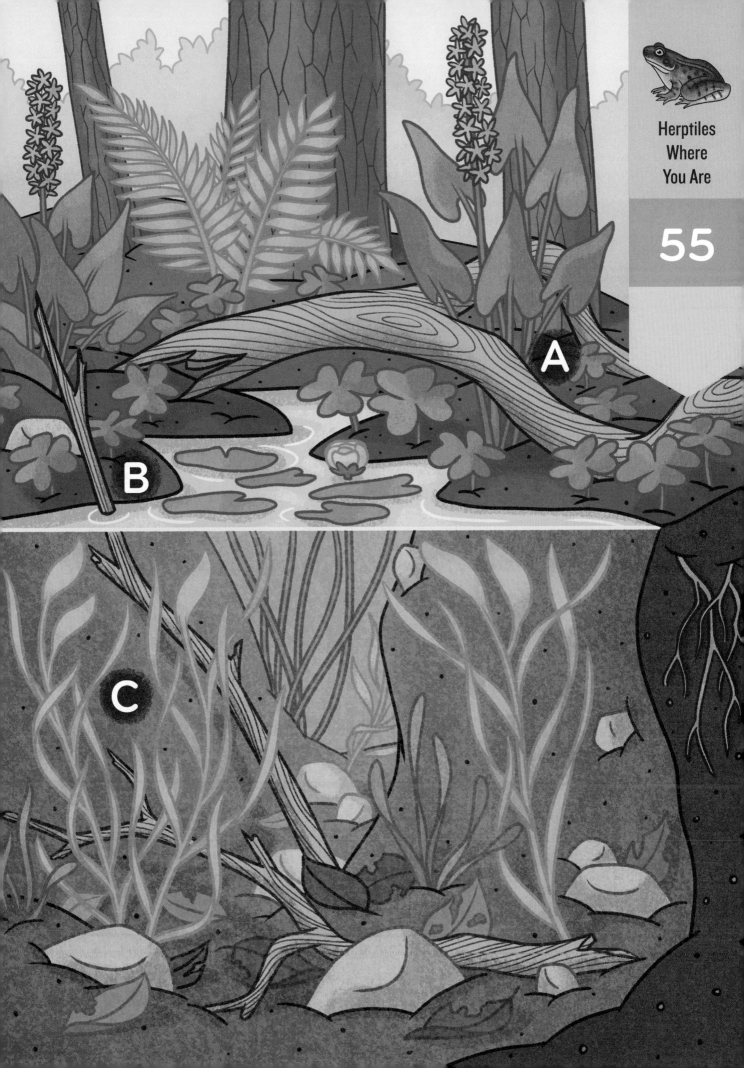

Herp Warm-Up & Cooldown

Because they are cold-blooded, or ECTOTHERMIC, herptiles rely on their environments to regulate their body temperatures. (*Ecto* means "outer" or "outside," and *thermic* means "heat.") Each of the herps on the next page have adapted to one of the habitats below.

Ocean

Wetland

Forest

Desert

➤ Each of these herps has a way of using their environment to maintain their body temperature. Write which habitat each herp belongs to on the line below.

A RED-BACKED SALAMANDER looks for a hiding place among cool, moist leaves.

A DIAMONDBACK RATTLESNAKE basks in the sun, slithering into the shade if it gets too hot.

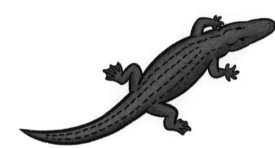

AN ALLIGATOR warms itself in the sun by the water.

A BULLFROG croaks with its head just above the water.

A LEATHERBACK SEA TURTLE only comes out of the water to lay its eggs.

A HORNED LIZARD burrows in the sand to cool off—or to keep warm.

Anatomy of a Reptile Egg

Reptiles are cold-blooded vertebrates that have lungs and scaly skin and that lay soft-shelled eggs on land. Reptiles were the first vertebrates to adapt to living on land. This was possible because their eggs have protective layers and a leathery shell so they don't dry out. Turtles, snakes, lizards, and alligators all lay eggs on land.

➤ Label the parts of the reptile egg on page 59, according to these hints:

- The developing reptile is the EMBRYO.

- The yellow YOLK SAC contains food that the baby reptile will absorb as it grows inside the egg.

- The AMNION is a bag of fluid that surrounds and protects the embryo.

- BLOOD VESSELS carry oxygen and carbon dioxide throughout the egg.

- The EGGSHELL has tiny holes that allow for air and moisture to travel in and out of the egg. It also protects the embryo.

Alligators keep their eggs warm and hidden inside a nest of decaying plant matter.

**Herptiles
Where
You Are**

59

Answer
key on
page 111

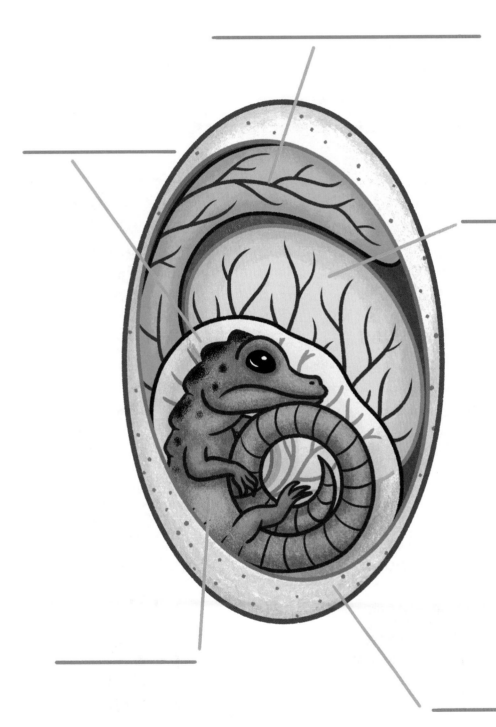

FUN FACT!

There are some reptile
species that don't
lay eggs but instead
give birth to live
young! These include
boa constrictors,
rattlesnakes, and
garter snakes.

Make an Alligator Egg

Many reptile eggs have a rubbery shell. To get a sense of how the shell might feel, try this experiment with a chicken egg.

YOU WILL NEED

1 chicken egg

Small pot

Slotted spoon

Small plate

Clear pint-size jar or cup

1½ cups vinegar

1 Put your egg in a small pot and add enough water to cover it. Bring the water to a boil, and boil the egg for about 7 minutes.

2 Remove the egg from the pot with a slotted spoon. Place it on a plate or towel and let it cool.

3 Gently place the egg in the clear jar. Pour the vinegar into the jar until the egg is completely covered.

4 Place the jar in the fridge for at least 3 days. You might want to put a lid on the jar so your fridge doesn't start to smell like vinegar. The vinegar will cause the calcium in the shell to dissolve, leaving the rubbery membrane.

5 Remove the egg from the jar with a spoon and place it on the plate. Touch it! How does it feel?

Adaptations for Survival

Herptiles have evolved many different ways of protecting themselves. Read about the examples below.

Many salamanders have bright colors to warn predators that they are poisonous to eat.

Some herptiles have venom.

Some herptiles use camouflage to hide from predators.

Turtles have structural defenses in the form of hard shells.

Geckos, like many salamanders and lizards, have the ability to lose their tails and regrow them. This is called regeneration.

Herptiles
Where
You Are

63

Answer
key on
page 111

What kinds of adaptations do these herptiles have
to protect themselves? Do they have **warning colors**,
venom, **camouflage**, **structural defenses**, or the ability to
regenerate body parts? Some may have more than one!

➤ *Write your best guess next to each animal.*

 Red-spotted newt

_____

_____

 Loggerhead sea turtle

_____

_____

Green tree frog

_____

Gila monster

_____

_____

Hunting for Herps

Finding herptiles can be a challenge. First, you need to figure out where they might be living. Here's one way to start exploring.

1   Go to Google Maps and type in your address.

2   Click on "satellite view."

3   Slowly start zooming out or panning left, right, up, and down. Look for potential herptile habitats such as wetlands, swamps, ponds, forests, or green spaces in your city or town.

4   If the land is accessible to you and it's safe to visit (for example, a nearby park), try going there to search for reptiles and amphibians.

List some places near you where you could hunt for herptiles:

_____

_____

_____

DON'T GET DISCOURAGED! While some herps may live only in particular habitats, others such as toads and garter snakes may be as close as a sidewalk or a potted plant. Keep your eye out for herps wherever you are! Here are a few hints to help your search. Turn the page for a chart to record what you find.

Tips for Finding Amphibians

- Amphibians are most easily found in water. In spring, look for egg masses in ponds or vernal pools.

- If you find egg masses, go back every week or so and look for tadpoles.

- Look for adult frogs around the edges of ponds, swamps, or marshes.

- Toads are often found in gardens or sandy soils.

- Salamanders can often be found in forests by turning over logs or rocks. Be sure to put the log or rock carefully back into place.

Tips for Finding Reptiles

- Aquatic turtles may be the easiest reptiles to see. They swim in ponds or lakes and come out to bask on rocks or logs on sunny days.

- Snakes and lizards also bask, so look for them in protected sunny locations, particularly on or near rocks.

- There are very few poisonous snakes in North America, but it is important not to approach any snake unless you are absolutely certain it is not poisonous.

- Alligators live in coastal wetlands from North Carolina to eastern Texas. Never approach an alligator, no matter how curious you are!

➤ On this page or in your field journal, keep a running list of the herptiles you see in your area.

What time of year do you see the most herptiles?

_____

Do you see more reptiles or amphibians?

_____

Herptile: _____ Date: _____

Location: _____

Observations: _____

_____

Herptile: _____ Date: _____

Location: _____

Observations: _____

_____

Herptile: _____ Date: _____

Location: _____

Observations: _____

_____

NATURALIST'S TIP

Amphibians can absorb potentially harmful chemicals such as bug spray and hand lotion through their skin. Keep that in mind before attempting to touch one!

Amphibian Sounds

Salamanders make no noises, but frogs sure do! The easiest way to find frogs is to listen for them in spring. Frogs call mostly in the evening or at night, but also on cloudy days.

➤ *Starting in early spring, listen for the peeps and croaks of the frogs in your local wetlands.*

How many different frog sounds do you think you can hear? _____

How would you describe them (low and creaky, high and shrill, etc.)? How big do you imagine the frogs are that make each sound?

_____

_____

_____

With practice, you can learn to recognize types of frogs by their calls. Go online to search for the kinds of frogs you might hear in your region. Based on your research, list three frog calls you can listen for where you live.

Example:

SPECIES: Spring peeper   CALL: Peep peep peep

SPECIES: _____   CALL: _____

SPECIES: _____   CALL: _____

SPECIES: _____   CALL: _____

BE A COMMUNITY SCIENTIST!

Help Out on a "Big Night"

One of the biggest challenges facing amphibians occurs during their spring trek to lay eggs in ponds and other wetlands. On warm, wet, early-spring nights, hordes of amphibians move from upland habitat down to the ponds to mate. These nights are called BIG NIGHTS. During this time, many frogs and salamanders are at risk while crossing roads.

Many local nature centers and conservation groups offer programs around this time of year to celebrate amphibian migrations and help communities work together to protect these important animals. Call your local nature center to learn if they offer any opportunities to help these animals get across the roads safely!

You can also explore FROGWATCH USA online at akronzoo.org/frogwatch to learn how to identify and report frog calls in your area.

CLIMATE CONNECTION

Amphibians and their wetland habitats are particularly vulnerable to changes in weather patterns due to climate change. In some parts of the country, storms are becoming more severe and bringing more rain, while other parts of the country are seeing longer periods with no rainfall. Amphibians that depend on wetlands for different life stages, from egg to adult, are struggling to adapt to their quickly changing environment. In many places, their populations are declining. Helping out on a Big Night really makes a difference to these creatures!

Birds Where You Are

A bird is an **endothermic** (warm-blooded) vertebrate that has feathers and a toothless beak or bill and that lays hard-shelled eggs. Other groups of animals have beaks or lay eggs, but only birds have feathers. Most but not all birds can fly. Scientists who study birds are called **ornithologists**.

Birds live just about everywhere, including where you live. Look around a little, and you are sure to spot a bird!

Bird Anatomy

To be able to identify birds, it's important to learn some basic bird anatomy. Study the bird diagram below. This is a general diagram and will not fit every bird species, but it is a good starting point for learning to recognize the characteristics of different birds.

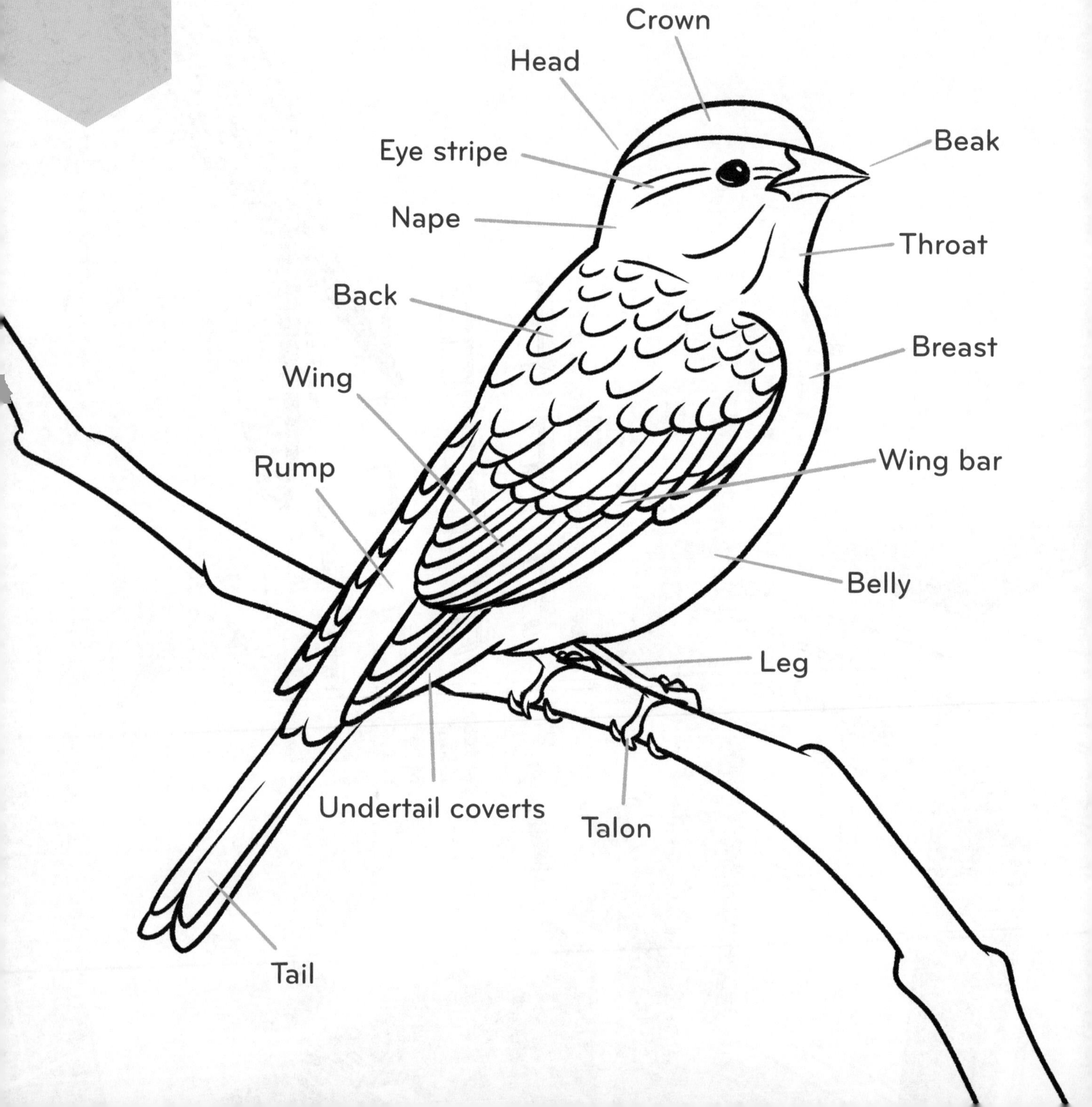

Crown

Head

Eye stripe

Beak

Nape

Throat

Back

Breast

Wing

Wing bar

Rump

Belly

Leg

Undertail coverts

Talon

Tail

What Bird Part Is It?

Now that you have studied the bird anatomy diagram, try to label some key identifying characteristics on the birds below.

Warblers by the Numbers

Every spring, thousands of small, brightly colored birds fly from south (where they spend the winter) to north (where they mate, build nests, and raise young). Some of these migrating birds are called warblers. There are many kinds of warblers, and they move quickly, often flitting around the tops of trees. You really have to study up on their details to be able to identify them.

➤ Practice noticing the different parts of a bird by coloring these male warblers "by the numbers."

BLACKBURNIAN WARBLER

○ No number = white
① Black
② Yellow
③ Orange
④ Gray
⑤ Brown

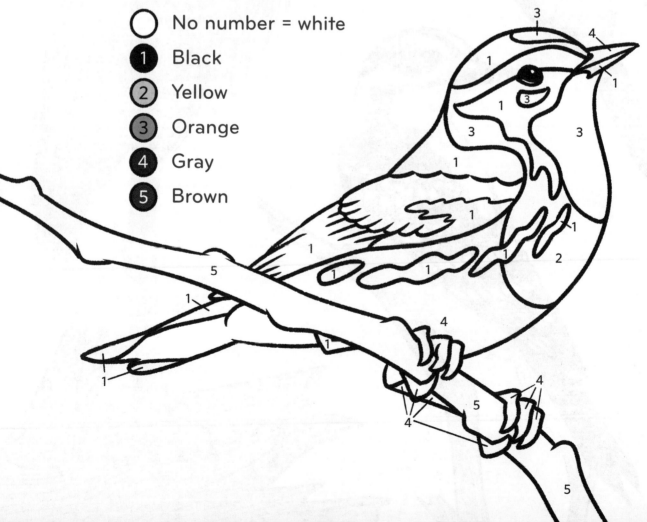

CHESTNUT-SIDED WARBLER

○ No number = white

① Black

② Yellow

③ Light yellow

④ Mahogany

⑤ Gray

⑥ Brown

FUN FACT!

Warblers are among the birds known as "songbirds" because of the beautiful sounds they make.

Tune Your Ear

Birds make sounds to attract mates, announce they are there, claim mating territory, and communicate warnings to other birds. Their vocalizations can be a song (musical series of phrases), a call or chip note (non-musical), or an alarm (urgent warning call).

Birds make their songs and calls with the help of a syrinx, the vocal organ of a bird.

chick-a-dee-dee-dee

JAY!

Birdsongs are also one way that people identify birds. The call of some birds actually sounds like their name. Listen to some recordings of bird vocalizations at allaboutbirds.org.

Make a Bird Sound Map

Find a place in your neighborhood where you hear birds. Settle into a comfortable spot where you can be still and listen. Now you're ready to make your Bird Sound Map.

GARDEN

SONG

PATH

QUACK QUACK

ME

POND

TAP TAP TAP

TREE

CAW!

SHRUB

1. Using the space on the back of this page, mark your location and add some features to help orient you (for example, a large tree, a swing set, a body of water).

2. For each bird sound you hear, note its location relative to your position. Is it to the left of you, right of you, above you?

3. Make a shape to represent the type of bird sound. Is it a call, an alarm, a song? Does it flow, or is it choppy?

NATURALIST'S TIP

You will see and hear more songbirds in the early part of morning and evening. During the day, many birds rest, staying sheltered and hidden from sight.

Your Bird Sound Map

Follow the instructions on the previous page to make your own sound map. How many different bird sounds did you hear? Did you hear songs, calls, alarms, or a combination?

NATURALIST'S TIP

Try sound mapping during different times of the day and different times of the year. You can also make sound maps that include sounds made by weather, traffic, other wildlife, and people!

Bird Silhouettes

Knowing birds' shapes and their silhouettes can help you figure out the kind of bird you are looking at even if you can't make out some of its more detailed characteristics.

➤ After studying the silhouettes below, turn the page to test your memory.

DOVE

HAWK

GOOSE

CROW

WOODPECKER

SONGBIRD

DUCK

HUMMINGBIRD

OWL

HERON

GULL

Match the Silhouettes

Now that you have studied the shapes of some common birds, try labeling them in this scene without flipping back to the guide.

Bird Adaptation Crossword

Time to learn some cool bird vocab! Using websites and books, try to solve this birdy crossword puzzle.

Birds
Where
You Are

79

Answer
key on
page 111

8 ACROSS: I R I D E S C E N T

ACROSS

4. Describing a species that moves from one region or habitat to another according to the seasons

5. Fleshy covering at the base of the beak

8. Showing bright colors that seem to change when viewed from different angles

9. A bird that eats only or mainly insects

10. Empty inside, making bird bones lighter for flying

11. Tuft of feathers on the head

DOWN

1. Bird feet with two toes in front and two in back

2. To groom one's feathers

3. The regular shedding of old feathers

6. To sit on eggs with the intent of hatching them

7. A bundle of bones, fur, and other indigestible parts regurgitated by a bird of prey

Bird Sketch

Find a place to observe birds of any kind. This might be at a window where you can see a bird feeder, in a city park, in a yard, or on the seashore. Try to observe one bird closely.

What is your bird doing? (Is it flying, hopping, perching, singing?)

Can you infer anything about your bird's actions? (Is it looking for food, nesting materials, or a mate?)

➤ Sketch your bird here. Remember to apply what you have learned about shape, color, and key characteristics. Can you match your bird to one in a field guide?

Eating like a Bird

What are some of your favorite snacks?

Depending on the bird species and where they live, birds can eat a variety of foods, from seeds, nuts, and fruits to insects, small mammals, other birds, and fish. Many birds eat different things at different times of the year. To fuel up for a long migration or to survive a cold winter season, **some birds eat at least the equivalent of their body weight in a day!**

➤ **What would YOU have to eat to consume the same amount as your body weight in a day?**

Your weight: _____

How many of each of the following foods would you need to eat if you were a bird fueling up for a long migration?

How many ¼-pound hamburgers? _____

How many 16-ounce bags of granola? _____

How many 4-pound trout? _____

Look on the package of a favorite snack to find the weight of a single serving, or use a kitchen scale. How many would you have to eat to equal your body weight? _____

Bird Words

Choose a favorite bird or a bird that you have recently observed. You can also head outside to observe a bird right now! Write down at least 10 descriptive words about your bird. Include its appearance (size, shape, color, pattern), its behavior, its sounds, and its habitat.

➤ **Brainstorm your bird words here:**

NOW, WRITE AN ACROSTIC POEM with the title "MY BIRD." An acrostic poem is when each line of the poem begins with a letter from the poem's title. Be sure to use the descriptive words you just brainstormed, but don't say what kind of bird you are writing about. Share your poem with friends or family. Can they guess what kind of bird your poem is about?

M _____

Y _____

B _____

I _____

R _____

D _____

Makes a high chirping sound.
You see it at the bird feeder.

Bright yellow with black cap and wings!
It looks like it soaked up the yellow spring sun.
Ready to fly!
Do you see the white wing bars?

(It's an American goldfinch! Did you guess?)

NATURALIST'S TIP

Try writing more acrostic bird poems in your field notebook. Use the bird's name, or come up with another creative title!

Birds as Builders

Birds need nests to shelter and protect their eggs and hatchlings. Different species of birds make nests with many different materials: sticks, stems, leaves, sand, mud, pine needles, moss, hair or fur, bark, spiderweb silk, and more! Birds nest on the ground, in the branches of living trees and shrubs, in holes and cavities in both living and dead trees, on buildings and other structures, and in nest boxes that people provide. Here are a few examples.

Bald eagles build huge nests of sticks lined with grass and moss.

Hummingbirds build tiny nests out of thistle or dandelion down held together by spider silk.

FUN FACT!

Bald eagles add to their nest each year. It may get to weigh more than a ton!

Robins build with dried grass and twigs held together with mud.

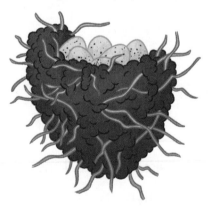

Barn swallows make nests of mud attached to a wall or beam.

NOW IT'S YOUR TURN TO TRY YOUR HAND AT NEST MAKING! Head outside to gather natural materials. You may want to start with a base structure such as a paper bag or bowl. You can also incorporate some arts and crafts items, but it's fun to use mud as glue, just like a bird! You can use yarn the same way a bird would use a fine twig or a piece of string.

➤ Draw a plan for your nest. What materials will you use? How will you put it together?

NOW TEST THE STURDINESS OF YOUR NEST by creating stormy conditions. Try blowing on it, lightly pouring water on it, or dropping it on the ground as if it had been blown from a tree. Did your nest hold together?

Bird Behavior Scavenger Hunt

Head outside to observe bird behavior! Keep in mind that you might not check off every box during just one walk, or even during one season. In fact, you will have to visit a few different habitats throughout the year to find everything in this scavenger hunt. Enjoy the challenge!

☐ Perching birds

☐ Molted feathers

☐ Berries

☐ Bird collecting nest materials

☐ Food for an insectivore

☐ Singing bird

☐ Hiding bird

☐ Wading bird

☐ Raptor prey

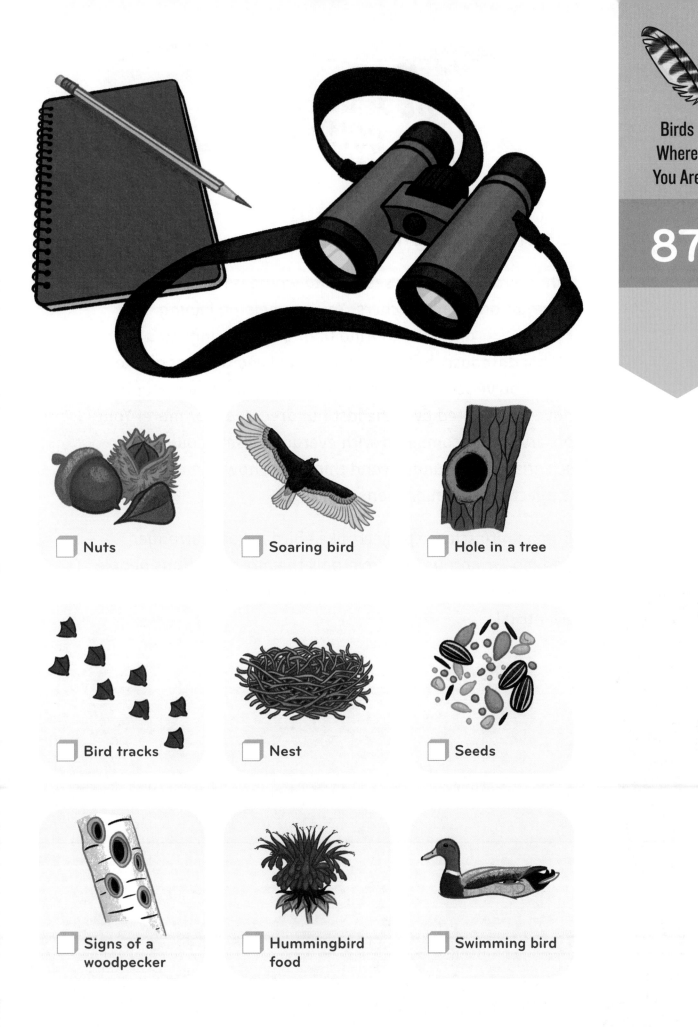

☐ Nuts

☐ Soaring bird

☐ Hole in a tree

☐ Bird tracks

☐ Nest

☐ Seeds

☐ Signs of a woodpecker

☐ Hummingbird food

☐ Swimming bird

BE A COMMUNITY
SCIENTIST!

Share Your Bird Sightings

What birds people are seeing and where is important information for researchers. You can help by joining eBIRD.ORG and contributing your bird sightings to a global database. With eBird you can keep track of all the birds you've seen and explore the data that other people have contributed over the last hundred years or more! Your observations, combined with everyone else's, could help scientists better understand things like how climate change is affecting bird migrations.

Community science projects like eBird become stronger and more rigorous research tools the more sightings people contribute. There can never be too many community scientists!

CLIMATE CONNECTIONS

Where a bird lives depends a lot on the climate and weather patterns it is adapted to. For example, the black-capped chickadee can be found across the northern United States, while the Carolina chickadee is found in the southeastern US. As the winters have gotten warmer, the Carolina chickadee has expanded its range farther and farther north. The same thing is happening to many other bird species around the globe—as our winters get warmer, the birds are moving northward.

Migrating birds depend on the right foods being available at the right times in the places they are migrating to. Climate change has caused changes in seasonal timing so the caterpillars, seeds, or other primary foods of migrating birds may not be available when the birds need them.

Mammals Where You Are

Mammals are **endothermic** (warm-blooded) vertebrates that have fur, give birth to live young, and produce milk to feed their young. Newborn mammals are not able to live on their own. They need protection and their mother's milk to survive and grow.

Some mammals have been domesticated by humans and live on farms or as pets in our homes. Other mammals do very well living close to humans—raccoons, squirrels, rabbits, skunks, deer, and coyotes, for example. Many other mammals, like wolves, mountain lions, moose, and elk, need much more room to roam. They tend to live in areas where fewer humans live.

Of course, you are a mammal, too!

Find Your Biome

Different species of mammals can be found in just about every biome on the planet. BIOMES are large geographic areas defined by their particular climate and the plants and animals that live there. Take a look at the map of North America on the facing page. It is divided into seven major biomes.

➤ First, make a dot on the map where you live. Next, use the clues below to learn where each of the biomes is located on the map. Color the map to match the clues.

The coast of California is CHAPARRAL.

Northern Canada and Alaska are TUNDRA.

Just south of the tundra is the boreal forest, or TAIGA. It covers most of southern Canada.

The eastern part of the United States is TEMPERATE DECIDUOUS FOREST.

The central part of the United States, below the taiga, is GRASSLAND.

The most western section of the Pacific Northwest is TEMPERATE RAIN FOREST.

The western United States and northern Mexico are DESERT.

The most southern tip of Florida, the Caribbean islands, Central America, and part of Mexico are TROPICAL RAIN FOREST.

What biome do you live in? _____

_____

Can you list some mammals that live in your biome?

_____

_____

_____

FUN FACT!

Mammals can be large or small. The largest animal on Earth is the blue whale, measuring up to 98 feet long and weighing up to 400,000 pounds. The pygmy shrew is 2 inches long and weighs 0.15 ounce.

**Mammals
Where
You Are**

92

Answer
key on
page 111

Fuzzy Adaptations

Mammals have fur or hair, an adaptation that helps them survive in a variety of ways:

- INSULATION. Fur provides a protective layer and insulates the animal from both extreme cold and heat. It can even be waterproof!

- SENSING. Specialized hairs and whiskers help some mammals get information about their environment.

- CAMOUFLAGE. The color and patterns of a mammal's fur may help it blend into its habitat.

- WARNING. Fur color can also serve as a warning to predators.

- PROTECTION. Sharp quills are actually modified hairs.

➤ Study each animal's "hairy" adaptation. Then write in the function of that adaptation, choosing from the list above.

MOUSE

ADAPTATION: Whiskers

FUNCTION: *Sensing*

SKUNK

ADAPTATION: Fur colors

FUNCTION: _____

SHORT-TAILED WEASEL (summer/winter)

ADAPTATION: Changing fur colors

FUNCTION: _____

Mammals
Where
You Are

93

Answer
key on
page 111

PORCUPINE

ADAPTATION: Quills

FUNCTION: _____

POLAR BEAR

ADAPTATION: Hollow hair

FUNCTION: _____

BEAVER

ADAPTATION: Double layers of fur

FUNCTION: _____

The Amazing Opposable Thumb

Like all mammals, humans have many amazing adaptations. One adaptation that we share with other primates is the opposable thumb.

Think about what you do with your hands every day, from the time you wake up in the morning to when you go to sleep at night.

➤ **List five ways that you use your thumbs.**

1. _____

2. _____

3. _____

4. _____

5. _____

NOW CHOOSE one of the activities you listed above and write it in the blank below to complete the investigation question. Then try the experiment on the next page!

"Can I _____ faster with or without my thumbs?"

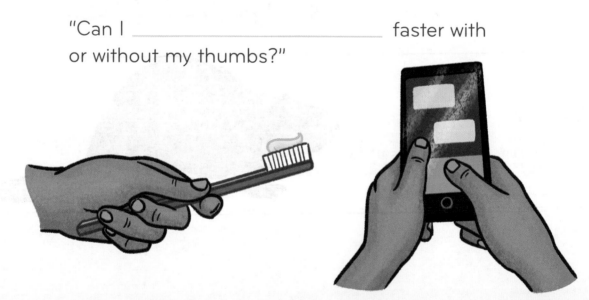

Timed Thumb Experiment

Based on the activity you chose, conduct the following experiment to find out just how handy your thumbs really are! You will need masking tape and a timer or clock.

1. Time yourself doing your chosen activity as you usually would, using your thumb or thumbs. Run five tests, recording the time for each test in the table below. Then find the average of the five tests.

2. Next, using masking tape, tape your thumb or thumbs tightly to the side of your hand. You might need to ask a friend or family member to help make sure your thumb really cannot be used.

3. Time yourself doing the exact same activity with your thumb taped. As before, run five tests, recording your times and then finding the average.

	TEST 1	TEST 2	TEST 3	TEST 4	TEST 5	AVERAGE
Time with thumbs						
Time without thumbs						

Hint!
To get the average, add up all your times and then divide by 5.

What were the results of your investigation? What makes our thumbs such a useful adaptation?

_____

_____

FOR FUN: If you didn't choose to tie your shoes or brush your teeth for this experiment, try them without thumbs and see how you do!

Hunter or Hunted?

Some mammals are predators, and some mammals are prey. By noticing a mammal's eye locations and the shapes of its teeth, you can determine which it is. If an animal has its eyes on the front of its head, it is usually a predator. If the eyes are on the sides of the head, it is usually a prey animal. Look at the illustration below.

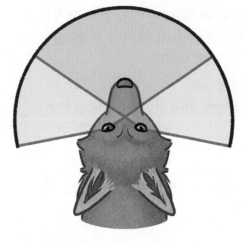

The frontal fields of vision seen by both eyes overlap, helping the predator focus on prey.

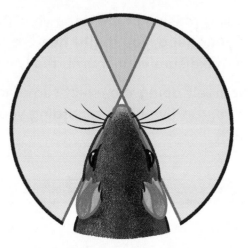

The wide field of vision seen by each eye helps the prey animal see what's coming.

REMEMBER, HUMANS ARE PREDATORS—just take a look at where your eyes are positioned! If you have pets, take a look at their eyes. Are they predator or prey?

➤ Write *predator* or *prey* under each of the pets below.

Change Your Point of View

Try this simple trick to see what it might be like to be a prey animal. Place a ruler or two of your fingers on the bridge of your nose to limit your field of vision. Close one of your eyes. Rotate your head to see how it feels to have this limited view. Switch eyes. Now take the ruler away and use your "predator" eyes again. Do you notice the difference?

Do you think it would be easier or harder to hunt with your "prey" eyes?

Do you think it would be easier or harder to see if another animal is approaching?

What other adaptations do predators and prey have to help them hunt or help them avoid being hunted? (Hint: Think feet, claws, and ears.)

NATURALIST'S TIP

Here's a simple rhyme to help you remember: Eyes on the front, the animal hunts. Eyes on the side, the animal hides.

Mammal Observation Study

Find a safe spot near some shrubs or trees or in a field where you can sit quietly, and be patient. Near a bird feeder or compost pile might be a good place to observe as well. Depending on where you are, you might see a squirrel, chipmunk, raccoon, or even a deer. Once you have found a good observation station, spend time observing a mammal (or group of mammals) at least two different times.

➤ Use the investigation sheet below to take notes while you observe. For each behavior, try to record how often the animal does it.

ANIMAL/TIME OBSERVED	MOVEMENTS	FEEDING
EXAMPLE: Gray squirrel 5 min.	Sitting—4 times Running—most of the time Tail flicking—8 times Jumping—once	Foraging—2 times Feeding—never Storing—buried one acorn Digging—2 storage attempts

NATURALIST'S TIP

Keep in mind that animals are most active around sunrise or sunset. Many will hide when they hear or see people. You may be able to see them only if you remain still and are very quiet.

INTERACTIONS	NOTES AND OBSERVATIONS
Chasing—one other squirrel, 3 times Scolding—4 times Fighting—never	

Toes, Heels & Claws

While snow makes a great place to find animal tracks, you can also find tracks in places with wet mud or sand. The first step to identifying animals by their tracks is to learn some of the specific characteristics of different families of mammals. Here are some questions to ask when you see a track.

HOW BIG IS IT? Tiny as a mouse's foot, or big as a bear's?

HOW MANY TOES? What shape are the toes?

Two toes = hooved animals, like deer, elk, moose, and cows

Four toes = canines (dogs), felines (cats), lagomorphs (rabbits, hares, pika)

Four toes in front paw, **five toes** in hind paw = rodents (mice, squirrels, beavers, porcupines)

Five toes = weasels, bears, raccoons, opossum

ARE THE CLAWS VISIBLE IN THE TRACK? Canine tracks often show claws, while feline tracks do not.

NATURALIST'S TIP

You may want to look online for downloadable guides to tracks for your state or region!

Mammals
Where
You Are

101

Answer
key on
page 112

➤ Using the information on the previous page,
fill in the blanks to identify the tracks below.
Choose from: BOBCAT, MOOSE, BLACK BEAR, and
RACCOON. Note that the length of each track is
given, but they are not drawn to scale!

4½"–5½"

Deer
2½"–3"

1⅞"

Snowshoe hare
Hind: 5"   Front: 2"

Red fox
Hind: 2"   Front: 2¼"

Hind: 4"   Front: 2½"

Gray squirrel
Hind: 2¼"   Front: 1½"

Hind: 7"   Front: 4½"

Make a Track Tunnel

To learn what species of small mammals live in your neighborhood or garden, you can make a track tunnel. The cardboard tunnel shelters your tracks from rain and makes the space feel safer to animals. If you don't have much luck in one spot, try another!

YOU WILL NEED

- ☐ Baking tray
- ☐ Fine, dampened sand or flour
- ☐ Ruler
- ☐ Bait (small, cut-up pieces of fruit and vegetables, birdseed, oatmeal, dog or cat food)

- ☐ Small low-sided dish
- ☐ Piece of cardboard large enough to make a small tent over your tray
- ☐ Track guide

1 Fill the baking tray with damp sand. Smooth out the surface with the ruler. Check to see that you can make a print with your fingers.

2 Place your bait in the dish in the middle of the tray.

3 Place the tray outside near a bush, garden, or any place an animal might take shelter.

4 Fold the cardboard in half to make a tunnel. Place it over the tray, and leave the tray overnight.

Mammals by Diet

Mammals can be herbivores (animals that eat plants), carnivores (animals that eat animals), or omnivores (animals that eat both plants and animals).

➤ Fill in the Venn diagram with the mammals listed by placing them in the correct category according to what they eat. Not sure? Look it up!

Rabbit	Coyote	Manatee	Bear
Woodchuck	Bobcat	Squirrel	Dog
Deer	Weasel	Opossum	Raccoon
Porcupine	Seal	Red fox	Horse

HERBIVORES   **OMNIVORES**   **CARNIVORES**

Mammals
Where
You Are

104

Answer
key on
page 112

Scat Stories

Naturalists use the word SCAT to refer to wild animal poop. Animal scat is another great clue to what kind of wildlife lives in your neighborhood. You can use scat to identify an animal as well as what it eats and where it travels.

➤ Study the scat drawings on page 105 and see if you can answer the questions based on the size, shape, and contents of the poop.

Which animals leave scat that looks like pellets?

Which animals leave scat that looks like grains of rice?

Which animals eat furry animals?

Which animal leaves scat that looks like it's made of wood chips or sawdust?

Which animal eats shelled animals?

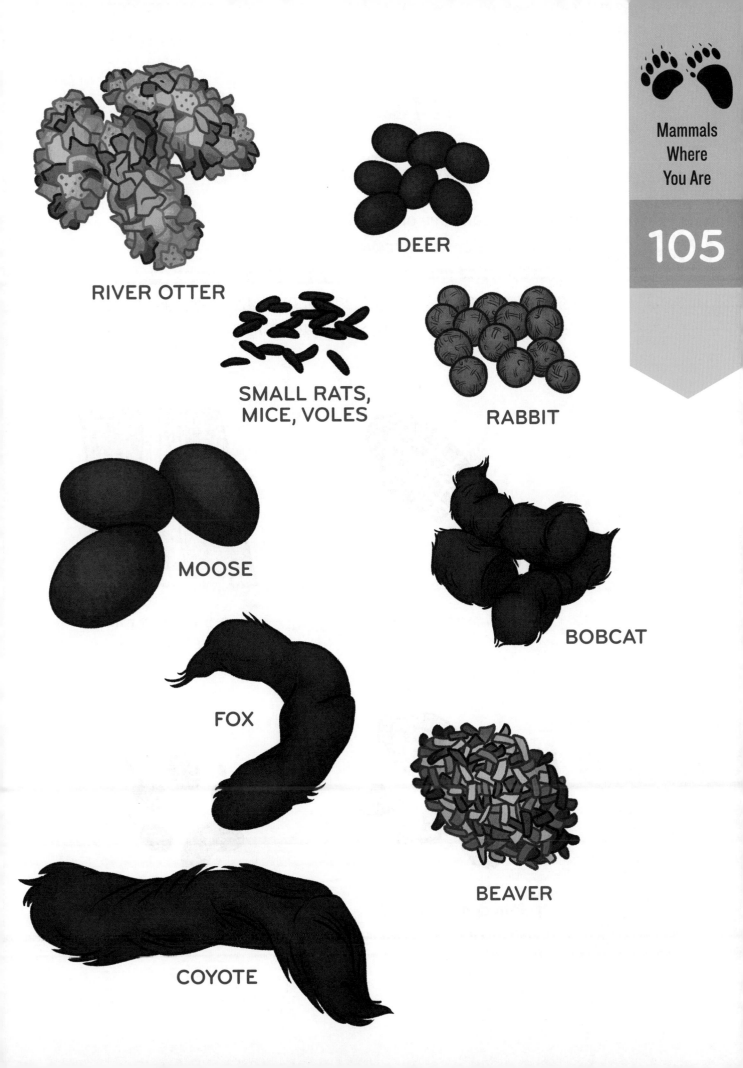

RIVER OTTER

DEER

SMALL RATS,
MICE, VOLES

RABBIT

MOOSE

BOBCAT

FOX

BEAVER

COYOTE

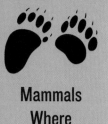
Mammal Sign Scavenger Hunt

Even if you can't see or hear a mammal, you can often observe the signs they leave in their habitats. Whenever you are outside exploring, look for mammal signs! You may not find all of the signs below, but if you keep your eyes open, you are sure to see some of them . . .

☐ **Human shoe print**

☐ **A hole that might be a home**

FUN FACT!

Red squirrels leave a pile of cone scales, called a midden, where they have been eating the seeds out of the cones.

☐ **Pinecone stripped by a squirrel**

☐ **Animal track**

☐ Beaver-chewed stump

☐ Mole or gopher hill

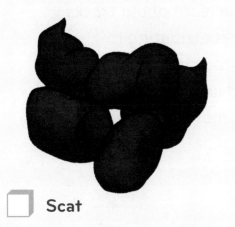

☐ Scat

☐ Chewed or torn twigs

FUN FACT!

Twigs browsed by deer look torn or shredded because deer have no upper incisors.

☐ Fur caught on a fence or bush

☐ Flattened grass where a mammal walked through

BE A COMMUNITY SCIENTIST!

Join the North American Animal Tracks Database

Because mammals can be hard to spot, they are less often included in community science projects. You can help change that! While you're out finding signs of mammals, document and share the tracks you find on iNATURALIST and join the NORTH AMERICAN ANIMAL TRACKS DATABASE. This project will help you learn about tracks and join other community scientists contributing to scientific research about mammals. You can also search the database for specific species and look at the photos that other people have posted of animal signs they've seen near them.

CLIMATE CONNECTIONS

Most mammals are well adapted to their habitats and the seasonal changes that happen in them. Climate change is causing seasons to be more erratic. For mammals that are adapted to a cold, snowy winter, a warmer, rainy winter may mean they can't survive. When climate patterns change, this makes it hard for animals that depend on the timing of leaves opening, plants flowering, seeds or fruit maturing, and other animals (prey) migrating or emerging from overwintering. Mammals that hibernate or sleep during the winter are also affected by changes in temperature and amount of snowfall.

Staying Curious

This may look like the end of the book, but it's actually another beginning. The great thing about being a naturalist is that there is always more to explore. Remember to follow your interests and keep observing nature close to home.

Try taking your nature studies to the next level by generating SCIENTIFIC QUESTIONS about what you observe. A scientific question is TESTABLE, meaning you can design an INVESTIGATION for it and maybe even discover some answers.

Dive back into your explorations from each of the chapters. Was there a particular chapter or activity that made you ask lots of questions and want to learn more? Start there! Refine your scientific questions, develop hypotheses, and design your own investigations by using the worksheet you can find at storey.com/investigation-worksheet.

Remember, investigations often lead to more questions.

THAT'S SCIENCE! HAVE FUN EXPLORING . . .

Answer Key

PAGE 10

```
C L M C H K N Q U M Y W N R A
O O I A N F H B U J U A O F Q
Q F L E G D P C W S H T U H
O I P O F N M O M W V E E R T
D E P D R Z I U E B F R B T B
E L Y H V E V F J Y F B O R R
V D M Y K C D X I N O O O S U
S G I K S H S P Q E E T K E L
G U I C B N F K E J R T G X E
S I H J A T A G S N D L R S R
U D J J Z M A C H E C E T G J
X E D O T M E S K P H I J O Z
R H D E T Z I R C S Q K L U S
F O I X Z P P E A C Z R F S H
H F I R S T A I D K I T W D H
```

PAGE 14

Observation or Inference?

- Ⓞ / I The plant is droopy.
- O / Ⓘ The plant needs more water.
- Ⓞ / I The bird is singing.
- Ⓞ / I The sky is cloudy.
- O / Ⓘ It is going to rain soon.
- Ⓞ / I The tracks in the sand have five toes.
- O / Ⓘ The grass is very wet because it rained.

PAGE 25

Skeletal system	Plant part: STEM OR TRUNK
Digestive system	Plant part: LEAVES, ROOTS
Integumentary system	Plant part: BARK

PAGE 31

```
F X T Q I P Y M O P I S T I L
P L O A V M W S B G P X T S R
G I O D V J O P T J L K F U
J F S W A K U C K I T F E N N
G S A T E N P J U J G A H B P
R M S U A R T E M Q H M W E B
A T E K R M G H T L N F A N U
I G J G G P E C E A D S N W D
U H Q R G Z O N T R L E P X T
S B P Y O Q W L J C P P G T E
B H O V A R Y Y L J O A L K D
F I L A M E N T E X L N R B
H T V M K D V F K Q N X V G I
R X O Z O S W B X B P M N R Z
E R I K G K Y I Q L Y Z B K J
```

PAGE 41

SEA SPONGE: 6	SPIDER: 2
WORM: 3	MILLIPEDE: 2
SNAIL: 1	LOBSTER: 2
SEA ANEMONE: 5	SEA STAR: 4

PAGE 44

Crossword:
1. ARTHROPOD
2. ANTS
3. SEGMENTED
4. PILLBUG
5. MILLIPEDE
6. METAMORPHOSIS
7. LOBSTER
8. SNAIL
9. SPIDER

PAGE 47

PAGE 54

TADPOLES: C
ADULT FROG: B
RED-BACKED SALAMANDER EGGS: A
AQUATIC ADULT NEWT: C
RED-SPOTTED NEWT EGGS: C
RED EFT: A

PAGE 57

FOREST

DESERT

WETLAND

WETLAND

OCEAN

DESERT

PAGE 59

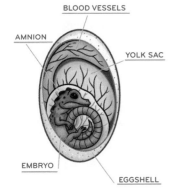

BLOOD VESSELS
AMNION
YOLK SAC
EMBRYO
EGGSHELL

PAGE 63

RED-SPOTTED NEWT
WARNING COLORS
REGENERATION

LOGGERHEAD SEA TURTLE
STRUCTURAL DEFENSE
CAMOUFLAGE

GREEN TREE FROG
CAMOUFLAGE

GILA MONSTER
WARNING COLORS
VENOM

PAGE 71

CROWN
BEAK
THROAT
HEAD
BACK
WING
BREAST
TAIL

PAGE 78

SONGBIRD
HAWK
WOODPECKER
HERON
OWL
GULL
GOOSE
DUCK
DOVE
CROW
HUMMINGBIRD

PAGE 79

4. MIGRATORY
5. CERE
8. IRIDESCENT
9. INSECTIVORE
10. HOLLOW
11. CREST

1. ZYGODACTYL
2. PREEN
3. MOLT
6. BROOD
7. PLUME

PAGE 91

PAGE 93

SKUNK
FUNCTION: WARNING

SHORT-TAILED WEASEL
FUNCTION: CAMOUFLAGE

PORCUPINE
FUNCTION: PROTECTION

POLAR BEAR
FUNCTION: INSULATION

BEAVER
FUNCTION: INSULATION

PAGE 96

PREDATOR, PREDATOR, PREY

PAGE 101

MOOSE

BOBCAT

RACCOON

BLACK
BEAR

PAGE 103

HERBIVORES   OMNIVORES   CARNIVORES

PORCUPINE   OPOSSUM   SEAL
MANATEE   BEAR   BOBCAT
DEER   RACCOON   WEASEL
RABBIT   SQUIRREL
HORSE   COYOTE
WOODCHUCK   RED FOX
DOG

PAGE 105

PELLETS: DEER, RABBIT, MOOSE

GRAINS OF RICE: SMALL RATS, MICE, VOLES

EAT FURRY ANIMALS: BOBCAT, FOX, COYOTE

WOOD CHIPS: BEAVER

SHELLS: RIVER OTTER